You Can't Over Medicate on the Word of God: Healing Scriptures

Dr. Micah Mitchell
www.micahandkerry.com

Table of Content

Forewords

Dr. Micah Mitchell is a prophetic and apostolic voice to his generation. He is an anointed leader who has a desire to see his generation impacted for and by, the power of God. He desires to see them walk in the fullness God has for them. He knows this is only possible through the power of the word of God, the anointing of the Holy Spirit, and an intimate relationship with the Father.

Dr. Micah Mitchell has both a revelation of the integrity of God's word as well as, how to apply it practically in ones' life. Having been diagnosed with a rare form of sinus cancer in 2012, (check the dates) he stood on the healing promises of scripture as the Lord manifested His healing power in his life. Upon being raised from being bedridden, he answered the call to proclaim the Gospel as a prophet to South Africa where he still lives today with his wife Kerry Mitchell, who works side by side in the ministry with him.

Dr. Micah and Kerry have traveled extensively both in the United States, South America and in several countries in South Africa. His love for, and knowledge of the word of God is evident in his preaching and teaching. Miracles, healing and signs and wonders follow their ministry. I wholeheartedly recommend both his ministry and this, his first publication, "You Can't Over Medicate On the Word Of God: Healing Scriptures". This book is a download from Heaven that I know will be a blessing to you and will transform your life!

Apostle Jason E. Mitchell
Waters of Hope International Ministries
Hammond, LA. USA

<u>Introduction</u>

These scriptures are meant to help you in your fight against whatever sickness you are facing. I used these scriptures when I was battling cancer and the after effects of it. I refused to let the report of the doctors stop me. I knew, just like you, that I had a destiny waiting to be birthed on the inside of me. If we accept and believe what the reports say we'll find ourselves sitting in a room rotting with a purpose on the inside of us.

The Word of God must become active and moving in our life. Every day the enemy is planting seeds in our life and feeding us lies. We must plant seeds of the Word that will overcome the lies. We do this by thinking correctly and believing what God says about us.

1. We must SPEAK the Word out loud. Faith, our reality, the way we perceive the world we live in comes by what we hear. That is why Jesus said, "Let thy KINGDOM COME", in a prayer. When we pray we speak our heart, but we also speak the Fathers heart. That is why we must pray the Word of God, because the Word is the heart of the Father. When we speak the Heart of the Father, His love is released. Love conquers everything!

2. We must MEDITATE on the Word of God. Check out: Joshua 1:9, Psalms 119:15, and Psalms 104:34. When we meditate we shift our minds on to GOOD THINGS. "Finally, brethren, whatever is true, whatever is honorable, whatever is right, whatever is pure, whatever is [a]lovely, whatever is of good repute, if there is any excellence and if anything worthy of praise, [b]dwell on these things." (Philippians 4:8) If we are constantly thinking about what "could" happen we will never see the impossible become possible. It won't come naturally, but over time it will spring up like living waters. It will get you through those days when you can't speak. All you can do is THINK about how God is your healer.

3. Write! I wrote these scriptures when I could, every day. Some days I could only write one scripture. I made it a point to get them on the inside of me. I love Deuteronomy 11:18, where it says to IMPRESS AKA WRITE them upon your heart. There is something about writing that ingrains it into our memory. You're not just saying something and hearing it, but you also must think about writing it. It causes you to think.

The last thing I want to tell you to do, is write a confession for yourself. Look up scripture or take scripture from below and make it into a paragraph to a page. Everyday confess what God's word says for your life. There were days back then, still today, where I looked in the mirror and spoke it to myself.

The whole point of doing this isn't to "catch" or "get healed." Why do this then? I'm glad you asked! It's about falling deeper in love with Jesus. See, the Word is the love of Jesus active and moving in our life. As I release the Word over my health it begins to outweigh everything else. This causes you to believe so much in the Lover of your soul that you know, beyond a doubt, that He will show up. We have to get so lost in Jesus, and we do that by releasing the Word of God over our life.

Please, remember, I'm not telling you not to go to the doctor or take you medication. Use the scriptures below to help you defeat the adversary of your soul – the devil.

Scriptures

The scriptures are written as confessions to make them more personal. I changed the "you" to "I", etc. This built my faith, because I was claiming it for myself.

Faith
My belief system
What I believe to be true
My reality on earth
Comes from hearing, and hearing through the Word of Christ Jesus.
(Romans 10:17)

Bless the Lord, O my soul,
And all that is within me, bless His holy name.
Bless the Lord, O my soul,
I will not forget one of His benefits;
God has pardoned all my iniquities,
God has healed all my diseases;
God redeems my life from the pit,
God crowns me with lovingkindness and compassion;
God satisfies my years with good things,
So that my youth is renewed like the eagle.
My God performs righteous deeds
And judgments for all who are oppressed.
My God is compassionate and gracious,
My God is slow to anger and abounding in lovingkindness
(Psalm 103:1-6,8)

Blessed be the Lord, who daily bears me up;
God is my salvation.
(Psalm 68:19)

I will rejoice in the Lord,
I will be joyful in God my Savior.
The Sovereign Lord is my strength;
God makes my feet like the feet of a deer,
God enables me to tread on the heights
(Habakkuk 3:18-19)

Heal me, O Lord, and I shall be healed;
save me, and I shall be saved,
for You are my praise.
(Jeremiah 17:14)

It is time for the Lord to act,
For they have broken Your law.
(Psalm 119:126)

My help comes from the Lord,
Who made heaven and earth.
God will not let my foot be moved;
God who keeps me will not slumber.
The Lord is my keeper.
The Lord is my shade on my right hand.
The sun shall not strike me by day, nor the moon by night.
The Lord will keep me from all evil;
He will keep my life.
The Lord will keep my going out and my coming in.
From this time forth and forevermore.
(Psalm 121)

God is my refuge and strength, my very present help in
trouble.
Therefore, I will not fear though the earth gives way,
though the mountains be moved into the heart of the sea,

though its waters roar and foam, though the mountains
tremble at its swelling.
I will not fear, for God, the GREAT I AM,
is with me; I do not anxiously look about,
for God, the GREAT I AM, is my God.
God will strengthen me and surely God will help me.
Surely God will uphold me with His MIGHTY righteous
right hand.
(Isaiah 41:10/Psalm 46:1-3)

For I have made the Lord my refuge,
Even the Most High my dwelling place.
No evil will befall me,
Nor will any plague come near me.
(Psalm 91:9-10)

Because I love God,
Therefore, God will deliver me;
God will set me securely on high,
because I have known God's name.
I will call upon God, and God will answer me;
God will be with me in trouble;
God will rescue me and honor me.
With long life God will satisfy me
I will see the Salvation of the Lord.
(Psalm 91:14-16)

I will give earnest heed to the voice of the Lord, my God.
I will do what is right in God's sight.
I give ear to God's commandments.
I keep all of God's statutes.

God will not put any of the diseases on me, which He put
on the Egyptians.
For God, the Lord, is my healer.
(Exodus 15:26)

I will not die, but live,
And tell of the works of the Lord.
(Psalm 118:17)

I cried out to the Lord in my trouble,
and God delivered me from my distress.
God sent forth His Word and healed me and rescued me
from my pit and destruction.
(Psalm 107:19-20)

I will give attention to God's Words;
I will incline my ear to God's Sayings.
I will not let God's Words depart from my sight.
I will keep God's Words in the midst of my heart.
For God's Words are life to me,
I find them, and they are health to my body.
I keep guard over my heart with all diligence,
because from it flow the springs of life.
(Proverbs 4:20-23)

I will not be wise in my own eyes.
I fear the Lord and worship Him,
and turn entirely away from evil.
The fear of the Lord is health to my flesh
and refreshment to my bones.
(Proverbs 3:7-8)

Jesus Himself bore my sins in His body on the cross,
that I might die to sin and live in righteousness,

right standing with God.
Jesus' wounds have healed me.
(1 Peter 2:24)

Blessed be the Lord who has given rest to me,
according to all that He has promised me.
Not one Word has failed of all of God's good promises,
which He spoke by Moses His servant.
(1 Kings 8:56)

All my grief's Jesus Himself bore.
And all my sorrows Jesus carried.
Jesus was pierced through for my transgressions.
Jesus was crushed for my iniquities.
The chastening for my well-being fell upon Him,
And by His stripes I am healed.
(Isaiah 53:4-5)

I will serve the Lord my God.
God shall bless my bread and water,
God will take sickness from my midst.
I will not lose my dreams or visions to miscarriage or be
barren in Zion.
God will always fulfill the number of my days.
(Exodus 23:25-26)

The enemy comes only to steal and kill and destroy.
Jesus, my Redeemer, my Salvation,
came so that I may have life,
and have it more abundantly.
(John 10:10)

As the heavens are higher than the earth,
so are God's ways higher than my ways

and God's thoughts higher than my thoughts.
For as the rain and snow come down from the heavens,
and return,
watering the earth and making it bring forth and sprout,
that it may give seed to the sower and bread to the eater,
so shall God's words be that come from His mouth:
it shall not return to me void,
but it shall accomplish that which God pleased and
purposed, and it shall prosper.
(Isaiah 55:9-11)

For God will restore my health
God will heal me of all of my wounds
(Jeremiah 30:17)

Christ redeemed me from the curse of the Law, He became
a curse for me.
(Galatians 3:13)

God has not given me a spirit of fear, but of power and
love and discipline.
(2 Timothy 1:7)

I hold fast the confession of my hope without wavering,
for God who promised is faithful.
I am confident; that God has begun a good work in me and
will perfect it until the day of Christ Jesus' return.
(Hebrews 10:23, Philippians 1:6)

I will not die, but live,
and tell of the works of the Lord.
(Psalm 118:17)

Now faith is my assurance of things hopcd for,
and my conviction of things not seen.
By faith I understand that the worlds were prepared by the
Word of God,
so that what is seen was not made out of things which are
visible
(Hebrews 11:1-3)

By faith even Sarah herself received the ability to
conceive,
even beyond the proper time of life,
since she considered God faithful to His promises.
(Hebrews 11:11)

Therefore, since I have so great a cloud of witnesses
surrounding me.
I will lay aside everything that encumbrances me
And the sin which so easily entangles me.
I run with endurance the race that is set before me.
I fix my eyes on Jesus, the Author and Perfecter of my
faith,
Who for the joy set before Him endured the cross,
despising the shame, and has sat down at the right hand of
the throne of God.
For Jesus who has endured such hostility by sinners
against Himself,
so that I will not grow weary nor lose heart.
(Hebrews 12:1-3)

I confidently say, "The Lord, Jesus, is my helper, I will not
be afraid. What will man do to me?"
(Hebrews 13:6)

I believe in Jesus.
These signs will follow me:
In Jesus' Name I will cast out demons.
I will speak in new tongues.
I will pick up serpents with my hands.
If I drink any deadly poison, it will not hurt me
I will lay my hands on the sick, and they will recover.
(Mark 16:17-18)

This is my confidence, which I have in Jesus,
that, if I ask anything according to His will, He hears me.
I know that He hears me in whatever I ask,
I know that I have the requests, which I have asked of
Him.
(1 John 5:14-15)

In Jesus' Name, whatever I bind on earth it shall be bound
in heaven;
and whatever I loose on earth it shall be loosed in heaven.
(Matthew 18:18)

At the name of Jesus every knee will bow,
of those who are in heaven and on earth and under the
earth,
and that every tongue will confess that Jesus Christ is
Lord,
to the glory of God the Father.
(Philippians 2:10-11)

I say to the mountains in my life,
'Be taken up and cast into the sea,
and I will not doubt in my heart,
but believe that what I say is going to happen,
it will be granted to me.

(Mark 11:23)
Jesus Christ is the same yesterday and today and forever.
(Hebrews 13:8)

"The Spirit of the LORD is upon me,
Because He has anointed me
To preach the gospel to the poor;
He has sent me to heal the brokenhearted,
To proclaim liberty to the captives
And recovery of sight to the blind,
To set at liberty those who are oppressed;
(Luke 4:18)

Jesus of Nazareth,
God anointed Him with the Holy Spirit and with power
Jesus went about doing good and healing all who were
oppressed by the devil,
for God was with Him.
(Acts 10:38)

I believe in Jesus.
The works that Jesus did
I will also do,
Greater works I will do
God has sent me a Helper,
Holy Spirit,
Who is always with me.
I have the Spirit of truth, whom the world cannot receive,
because it does not see Him or know Him,
but I know Him because He abides within me.
(John 14:12,16-17)

I will ask, and it will be given to me;
I will seek, and I will find.
I will knock, and it will be opened to me.
(Matthew 7:7)

For though I walk in the flesh
I do not war according to the flesh
My weapons of my warfare are not of the flesh
They are divinely powerful for the destruction of evil
fortresses.
In Jesus' Name I am destroying every speculation,
Every lofty thing that rises up against the knowledge of
God.
I am taking every thought captive to the obedience of
Christ.
(2 Corinthians 10:3-5)

I have not seen the righteous forsaken nor it seed begging
for bread.
All day long I am gracious and lend, and my descendants
are a blessing.
(Psalm 37:25-26)

The God of peace sanctifies me entirely;
My spirit, soul, and body is preserved complete, without
blame at the coming of our Lord Jesus Christ.
(I Thessalonians 5:23)

The Lord is good,
My stronghold in the day of trouble.
God knows me - I take refuge in Him.
God with an overflowing flood, will make a complete end
to all of my adversaries
God will pursue all my enemies into darkness.

No trouble will rise-up a second time against me.
(Nahum 1:7-9)

I will be strong in the Lord and in the strength of His might.
I put on the full armor of God
I will be able to stand firm against the schemes of the devil.
For my struggle is not against flesh and blood,
but against the rulers, against the powers, against the world forces of this darkness,
against the spiritual forces of wickedness in the heavenly places.
Therefore, I take up the full armor of God
so that I will be able to resist in the evil day
and having done everything, I will stand firm.
I will stand firm, having girded my loins with truth.
I have put on the breastplate of righteousness,
and having shod my feet with the preparation of the gospel of peace,
and in addition to all, I take up the shield of faith
with which I will be able to extinguish all the flaming arrows of the evil one.
I take the helmet of salvation, and the sword of the Spirit, which is the Word of God.
(Ephesians 6:10-17)

It is God who is at work in me, both to do His will and to work for His good pleasure.
(Philippians 2:13)
I will dwell on these things:
Whatever is true
Whatever is honorable
Whatever is right

Whatever is pure
Whatever is lovely
Whatever is of good repute
if there is any excellence
if anything is worthy of praise
(Philippians 4:8)

Let the high praises of God be in my mouth, And a two-
edged sword in my hand,
(Psalm 149:6)

I have conquered the enemy by the blood of the Lamb and
by the word of my testimony.
(Revelation 12:11)

Surely God is my salvation; I will trust and not be afraid.
The Lord, the Lord himself, is my strength and my
defense;
God has become my salvation.
With joy, I will draw water from the wells of my salvation.
(Isaiah 12:2-3)

Blessed be the Lord, who daily bears me up;
God is my salvation.
(Psalm 68:19)
Now to God, who is able to do far more abundantly
beyond all that I can ask or think, according to the power
that works within me.
(Ephesians 3:20)

Sing to the Lord, bless His name;
Proclaim good tidings of His salvation from day to day.
(Psalm 96.2)

To You I shall offer a sacrifice of thanksgiving,
And call upon the Name of the Lord.
(Psalm 116:17)

I will give thanks to Him,
I bless His name.
For the Lord is good;
His lovingkindness is everlasting
and His faithfulness to all generations.
(Psalm 100:4-5)

I will extol You, my God, O King,
And I will bless Your name forever and ever.
Every day I will bless You,
And I will praise Your name forever and ever.
(Psalm 145:1-2)

Scriptures of Jesus' Healing Power

When the disciples brought to Jesus many who were demon-possessed; Jesus cast out the spirits with a word, and healed all who were sick. This was to fulfill what was spoken through Isaiah the prophet: "He Himself took my infirmities and carried away my diseases." (Matthew 8:16-17)

A leper came to Jesus and bowed down before Him, and said, "Lord, if You are willing, You can make me clean." Jesus stretched out His hand and touched him, saying, "I am willing; be cleansed." And immediately his leprosy was cleansed. (Matthew 8:2-3)

Now they came to Jericho. As He went out of Jericho with His disciples and a great multitude, blind Bartimaeus, the son of Timaeus, sat by the road begging. And when he heard that it was Jesus of Nazareth, he began to cry out and say, "Jesus, Son of David, have mercy on me!" Then many warned him to be quiet; but he cried out all the more, "Son of David, have mercy on me!" So, Jesus stood still and commanded him to be called. Then they called the blind man, saying to him, "Be of good cheer. Rise, He is calling you." And throwing aside his garment, he rose and came to Jesus. So, Jesus answered and said to him, "What do you want Me to do for you?" The blind man said to Him, "Rabboni, that I may receive my sight." Then Jesus said to him, "Go your way; your faith has made you well." And immediately he received his sight and followed Jesus on the road. (Mark 10:46-52)

Now He arose from the synagogue and entered Simon's house. But Simon's wife's mother was sick with a high fever, and they made a request of Him concerning her. So, He stood over her and rebuked the fever, and it left her. And immediately she arose and served them. When the sun was setting, all those who had any that were sick with various diseases brought them to Him; and He laid His hands on every one of them and healed them. (Luke 4:38-40)

And behold, there came a man named Jairus, and he was a ruler of the synagogue. And he fell down at Jesus' feet and begged Him to come to his house, for he had an only daughter about twelve years of age, and she was dying. But as He went, the multitudes thronged Him. Now a woman, having a flow of blood for twelve years, who had spent all her livelihood on physicians and could not be healed by any, came from behind and touched the border of His garment. And immediately her flow of blood stopped. And Jesus said, "Who touched Me?" When all denied it, Peter and those with Him said, "Master, the multitudes throng and press You, and You say, "Who touched Me?" But Jesus said, "Somebody touched Me, for I perceived power going out from Me.

Now when the woman saw that she was not hidden, she came trembling; and falling down before Him, she declared to Him in the presence of all the people the reason she had touched Him and how she was healed immediately. And He said to her, "Daughter, be of good cheer; your faith has made you well. Go in peace." While He was still speaking, someone came from the ruler of the synagogue's house, saying to Him, "Your daughter is dead. Do not trouble the Teacher." But when Jesus heard it, He answered him, saying, "Do not be afraid; only believe, and she will be made well." When He came into the house, He permitted no one to go in except Peter, James, and John, and the father and mother of the girl. Now all wept and mourned for her; But He said, "Do not weep; she is not dead, but sleeping." And they ridiculed Him, knowing that she was dead. But He put them all outside, took her by the hand and called, saying, "Little girl, arise." Then her spirit returned, and she arose immediately. And He commanded that she be given something to eat. (Luke 8:41-55)

Jesus called His twelve disciples together and gave them power and authority over all demons, and to cure diseases. Jesus sent them to preach the kingdom of God and to heal the sick. (Luke 9:1-2)

After this there was a feast of the Jews, and Jesus went up to Jerusalem. Now there is in Jerusalem by the Sheep Gate a pool, which is called in Hebrew, Bethesda, having five porches. In these lay a great multitude of sick people, blind, lame, paralyzed, waiting for the moving of the water. For an angel went down at a certain time into the pool and stirred up the water; then whoever stepped in first, after the stirring of the water, was made well of whatever disease he had. Now a certain man was there who had an infirmity for thirty-eight years. When Jesus saw him lying there, and knew that he already had been in that condition a long time, He said to him, "Do you want to be made well?" The sick man answered Him, "Sir, I have no man to put me into the pool when the water is stirred up; but while I am coming, another steps down before me." Jesus said to him, "Rise, take up your bed and walk." And immediately the man was made well, took up his bed, and walked. And that day was the Sabbath. (John 5:1-9)

Bible Confession

Bless the Lord, O my soul, and all that is within me, bless His holy name. Bless the Lord, O my soul, and forget none of His benefits; Who pardons all your iniquities, who heals all of my diseases; Who redeems my life from the pit, who crowns me with lovingkindness and compassion; Who satisfies my years with good things, so that my youth is renewed like the eagle. (Psalm 103:1-5) Blessed be the Lord, who has given rest to me, according to all that He has promised; not one word has failed of all His good promises, which He promised through Moses His servant to me. (1 Kings 8:56)

God sent His word and healed me, and delivered me from my destruction. (Psalm 107:20) My griefs Jesus Himself bore, and my sorrows Jesus carried. Jesus was pierced through for my transgressions, Jesus was crushed for my iniquities; The chastening for my well-being fell upon Him, And by His stripes (beating) I am healed. (Isaiah 53:4-5) I will serve the Lord my God; He shall bless my bread and water, and He will take sickness from my midst. I will not lose my dreams or visions to miscarriage or be barren in Zion; God is and will fulfill the number of my days. (Exodus 23:25-26) Because I have made the Lord my refuge, and the Most High my dwelling place, there shall be no evil near me, nor any plague or calamity come near my dwelling. (Psalm 91:9-10)

I will give attention to the Word of God; I will Incline my ears to His sayings. I will not let them depart from my sight; I will keep them in the midst of my heart. For it is life to me and health to my body. I will watch over my heart with all diligence, for from it flow the springs of life. (Proverbs 4:20-23) I will not fear, for God is with me; I will not be anxiously looking about, for God is with me. He will strengthen me, surely God will help me, and uphold me with HIS righteous right hand. (Isaiah 41:10)

As the heavens are higher than the earth, so are God's ways higher than my ways and God's thoughts higher than my thoughts. For as the rain and snow come down from the heavens, and return not there again, but water the earth and make it bring forth and sprout, that it may give seed to the sower and bread to the eater, so shall God's Word be that out from His mouth: it shall not return to me void, but it shall accomplish that which God pleased and purposed, and it shall prosper in the things for which God sent it. (Isaiah 55:9-11)

I will ask, and it will be given to me; I will seek, and I will find; I will knock, and it will be opened to me. (Matthew 7:7) Christ redeemed me from the curse of the Law, He became a curse for me. (Galatians 3:13) For though I walk in the flesh, I do not war according to the flesh, for my weapons of warfare are not of the flesh, but divinely powerful for the destruction of fortresses. In Jesus' Name, I am destroying every speculation and every lofty thing that raises up against the knowledge of God, and I am taking every thought captive to the obedience of Christ (2 Corinthians 10:3-5)

God has not given me a spirit of fear, but of power and love and discipline. (2 Timothy 1:7) I hold fast the confession of my hope without wavering, for God who promised is faithful. I am confident, that God has begun a good work in me and will perfect it until the day of Christ Jesus' return. (Hebrews 10:23, Phil. 1:6) I will not die, but live, and tell of the works of the Lord. (Psalm 118:17)

For wisdom and knowledge have been granted to me. And God will give me riches and wealth and honor, such as none of the kings who were before me have possessed, nor those who will come after me" (2 Chronicles 1:12)

It is not by my power and the might of my hand that I have gotten wealth. But by the Lord my God, for it is He Who gives me power to get wealth, that He may establish His covenant which He swore to my fathers. (Deuteronomy 8:17-18)

I say to the mountains in my life, 'Be taken up and cast into the sea,' and will not doubt in my heart, but believe that what I say is going to happen, it will be granted to me. (Mark 11:23) I am a good man, I will leave an inheritance to my children's children, And the wealth of the sinner is stored up for the righteous, I am the righteousness of God. (Proverbs 13:22)

I love those who love me; And those who diligently seek me will find me. Riches and honor are with me, Enduring wealth and righteousness. My fruit is better than gold, even pure gold, And my yield better than choicest silver. "I walk in the way of righteousness, In the midst of the paths of justice, to endow those who love me with wealth, that I may fill their treasuries. (Proverbs 8:17-21)

I am a blessed man who does not walk in the counsel of the wicked, nor do I stand in the path of sinners, nor do I sit in the seat of scoffers! I delight in the Law of the Lord, And on His Law I meditate day and night. I am like a tree firmly planted by streams of water, which yields its fruit in its season and its leaf does not wither; And in whatever I do, I prosper. (Psalm 1:1-3) I have not seen the righteous forsaken nor its seed begging for bread. All day long I am gracious and lend, and my descendants are a blessing. (Psalm 37:25-26)

I will be strong in the Lord and in the strength of His might. I put on the full armor of God, so that I will be able to stand firm against the schemes of the devil. For my struggle is not against flesh and blood, but against the rulers, against the powers, against the world forces of this darkness, against the spiritual forces of wickedness in the heavenly places. Therefore, I take up the full armor of God, so that I will be able to resist in the evil day, and having done everything, I will stand firm. I will stand firm, having girded my loins with truth, and I have put on the breastplate of righteousness, and having shod my feet with the preparation of the gospel of peace, and in addition to all, I take up the shield of faith with which I will be able to extinguish all the flaming arrows of the evil one. I take the helmet of salvation, and the sword of the Spirit, which is the Word of God. (Ephesians 6:10-17)

Now to God who is able to do far more abundantly beyond all that I can ask or think, according to the power that works within me. (Ephesians 3:20) It is God who is at work in me, both to will and to work for His good pleasure. (Philippians 2:13)

Let the high praises of God be in my mouth, and a two-edged sword in my hand, (Psalm 149:6) I will enter His gates with thanksgiving and into His courts with praise. I will give thanks to Him, I will bless His name. For the Lord is good; His lovingkindness is everlasting and His faithfulness to all generations. (Psalm 100:4-5)

39356964R00019

Made in the USA
Middletown, DE
20 March 2019